Anonymous

Fingal King of Morven

A Knight-Errant

Anonymous

Fingal King of Morven
A Knight-Errant

ISBN/EAN: 9783337293444

Printed in Europe, USA, Canada, Australia, Japan

Cover: Foto ©Thomas Meinert / pixelio.de

More available books at **www.hansebooks.com**

FINGAL

KING OF

MORVEN,

A

KNIGHT-ERRANT.

Aut famam sequere, aut sibi convenientia finge.
Hor. de art. poet.

Qui variare cupit rem prodigialiter unam,
Delphinum silvis appingit, fluctibus aprum.　　　Ibid.

LONDON:

Printed, and sold by A. Donaldson, at his shop near *Nor-*
folk-street, in the *Strand.*

MDCCLXIV.

FINGAL

KING OF

MORVEN,

A

KNIGHT-ERRANT.

SIR,

I HAVE at laſt peruſed TEMORA; and, in return to your commands, muſt frankly acknowledge, the more of theſe Galic poems, or, more properly, tranſlations of Galic poetry, I have ſeen, the more am I confirmed in my former ſentiments with regard to them. From their firſt appearance, you know, I preſumed to think, that no certain or ſatisfying judgment could be formed with regard to their real poetic merit, till the originals are given to the public, and preciſely in the form, ſhape, and ſize they bore when firſt collect-

ed,

ed, before they had undergone any variation,
or new arrangement whatever. This fame
poetic merit will, in my opinion, turn out very high, when the pieces are viewed in their
proper light, and confidered as that fpecies of
poetry, to which, I apprehend, they verily
belong, whatever æra of compofition may be
affigned them.

THAT the true æra has been widely mif-
taken, I am ftill inclined to believe. Thefe
Galic poems have always appeared to me replete with ideas, fentiments, manners, cuftoms, all along pofterior to the three firft centuries. If we judge by thefe marks, as I think
we muft, we fhall be obliged to curtail the age
of the poems by a great number of years.
Thefe marks, Sir, will bring down the æra
of compofition to the times of the Danifh invafions; nay, even to the ages of chivalry.

PRAY, Sir, call under your review the
mighty Trenmor, the firft of the heroic race,
with whofe deeds of wonder trufty tradition
has favoured us; view, I fay, Trenmor in
Denmark arrayed in his heavy mail of fteel,

his

his fcull-cap of the fame folid metal, covered over with fteel : caft your eye upon Lady Inibaca*, accoutred in the fame knightly array : obferve the hero killing the boar, fending abroad his horn, getting his choice in the combat, protecting his charming Inibaca againft the love of the proud and furly Corlo : remember the firft century is the time, Denmark the place, the north-weft of Scotland the hero's country : caft your attention to the accounts, given by the Roman hiftorian † of the Caledonians, their array and arms, at this very time : All thefe balanced, fay, Sir, does Trenmor bear the greater femblance of the Caledonian hero in the latter end of the firft century, or of the invincible champion, the moft courteous knight, twelve centuries later ? Are thefe the manners, thefe the arms, thefe the knightlike achievements of the more than half-naked Caledonians in thofe rude and early ages ?

THE fame hiftorian ‡, you know, informs us, that Agricola owed the beginning of his decifive victory over the Caledonians, who

* Fingal, b. 6.   † Tacitus.   ‡ Tacitus.

were

were wanting, fays he, neither in bravery nor
conduct, to their total want of defenfive armour, and the infufficiency of their weapons.
The hiftorian had thefe accounts from Agricola himfelf: fhall we prefer the authority of
our hiftorian, or that of a Galic tradition,
more than fixteen centuries old?

Can we imagine, that Trenmor, the invincible Trenmor, Vergobret of his nation, was
fo very courteoufly, I had almoft faid fantafti-
cally, engaged in deeds of chivalry, on the o-
ther fide of a wide tempeftuous fea, at the very time the Romans, under the command of
Agricola, were pufhing their firft conquefts
in Caledonia, flaughtering myriads of her braveft fons, and penning up the reft behind the
Clyde and the Forth?

Once more, Sir, would not Trenmor, covered over with fteel as he was, have been
much more hero-like engaged in the defence
of his country, with the immortal Galgacus,
than in flaying fwine in Lochlin? Why was
neither Trenmor, nor any of his illuftrious
houfe, on that field of battle? Never fure did
Caledonia

Caledonia more want the aid of fuch invincible prowefs, fuch folid array.

COME we now, Sir, to the great grandfon
of the mighty Trenmor, Fingal, I mean,
firft of heroes. Give, pray, what degree of
attention you pleafe to Fingal in his fentiments, manners, arms, and array: view him
on every fide, in his every achievement, every expedition, and pronounce as you fhall fee
caufe; Fingal the Caledonian hero, in the
third century; or the invincible champion,
the moft courteous knight, about the 13th
age.

FINGAL's firft exploit, as it ftands recorded
in the infallible folios of Galic traditions;
traditions ever venerable on account of their
many years, their hoary locks! traditions of
above fifteen hundred years of age, yet not
impaired by years! Fingal's firft exploit,
according to thefe moft venerable vouchers,
was truly worthy the great and magnanimous
king *.

* Fingal, book 3.

STARNO

Starno king of Denmark, at the head of a fleet and army, had dared to invade the kingdom of Morven; Fingal and his heroes vanquiſh him in battle, and take him priſoner. Morven's king moſt generouſly, moſt courteouſly reſtores the bloody invader to his ſhips.

Fingal after this, ſome time, how long we are not told *, inſidiouſly invited by the ungrateful, the treacherous Starno, makes his appearance at the court of Denmark. Starno intends his deſtruction: the lovely Agandecca becomes highly enamoured: ſhe hints to the ſtranger hero her pappa's bloody deſign. Fingal thus warned, *keeps on his guard; keeps on his arms of ſteel*. Before him all Lochlin fled or died. The lifeleſs corſe of the ill-fated Agandecca, ſavagely murdered by her brutal father, is by Fingal conveyed aboard his white-ſailed ſhip, tranſported from Lochlin to Morven's kingdom, and there piouſly entombed.

Fingal king of heroes, after this expedi-

* Fingal, book 3.

tion

tion to Lochlin, what time intervening is not said, we find feafting and exploiting at the court of Sarno King of the Orkneys *. No tragic work here enfues, as lately at the windy-halls of Gormal. The blooming Comala is indeed no lefs charmed with our hero, than Agandecca had been. The royal damfel, difguifed in armour like a young warriour, follows Fingal to Morven ; whether aboard the King's fhip, or what other, bards and traditions are equally filent. Fingal, upon his arrival in his own kingdom, difcovers Lady Comala to be what fhe really was. Becaufe of her beauty and romantic paffion, he courteoufly refolves to make her his wife : very unhappily for the loving damfel, ere he could find time to carry his generous defign into execution, word is brought, that Caracalla, eldeft fon of the great Roman Emperor Severus, at the head of a mighty army, is juft about invading Caledonia. The hero flies as on the wings of thunder +, and with the refiftlefs force of its bolt, to the defence of his country. His battalions, it would feem, were under arms, and ready to march. Inftantly,

---

* Comala.   † Ibid.

upon

upon his coming up, he overwhelms Caracalla and his army ; chafes them over the fields of their pride. Before the King's triumphant return, Comala is no more ; fhe has withdrawn to her cloud. He had left her upon a hill at fome diftance from the field of battle; one of his heroes, the moft malignant of men, had perfuaded the unfortunate damfel, that the King had fallen by the fword of the enemy : fhe could brook life no longer.

Thus far, Sir, you will fuftain my narrative juft: and I fhall as readily allow, that all this may make very good poetry; but, in my humble opinion, a fpecies of poetry much more ftrongly marked with the gigantic limbs and Gothic features of the romance, than the natural fymmetry, the milder lineaments of the genuine epic mufe.

Some learned gentlemen would fain, it feems, perfuade us to take all thefe fhining exploits for real hiftorical facts; but as fuch, methinks, they can never well be admitted.

For is it conceivable, that Fingal, from
his

his kingdom of Morven, allowing him what time you pleafe, could have muftered a force fufficient to defeat a Roman army, that had but a little before returned from over-running all Caledonia without battle? But fhould e-ven this be fuppofed, the authentic hiftory of thofe times interpofes its negative.

THE Roman hiftorians indeed inform us *, that Caracalla attended his father in his ex-pedition over Caledonia, and returned with him to York; that in a fhort time after they had got there, accounts came, that the Mœ-ats and Caledonians were all in uproar, and taking to arms; that, upon this piece of in-telligence, Severus affembled his troops, inti-mated his defign of their marching again in-to the enemies country †; and declared, his intentions were to have the barbarians cha-ftifed with the utmoft rigour; but that death prevented him. Thefe hiftorians do not fay, that Caracalla ever again returned to the Car-ron; they give us not the fmalleft ground to imagine, that he ever again fought any battle, or had any rencounter with any enemy what-

---

* Herodian.   † Dion.

ever,

ever, within the bounds of this ifland. On
the contrary, they tell us, that Caracalla, during his father's laft illnefs, was wholly em-
ployed in endeavouring to perfuade the aged
Emperor's phyficians, and moft trufted fa-
vourites, to haften his death; that Caracalla
at that time minded nothing elfe, but how
he might effectuate his father's death, and
fupplant his brother Geta. And, inftead of
faying with the differtator *, that the news
of his father's death was brought him, after
he had undertaken this expedition, when he
had fcarce entered the enemies country; a con-
temporary hiftorian †, himfelf at that very
time a Roman fenator, informs us, that Caracalla was with his father in his laft mo-
ments, and gives us the dying words of this
great Emperor to his two fons, Caracalla and
Geta. But, Sir, tho' we fhould adopt the
differtator's narrative, we cannot imagine that
Caracalla returned again to the Carron : for
if the news of his father's death reached him,
when he had fcarce entered the enemies country, he muft have had thefe accounts juft as
he paffed the Northumbrian wall, as on the

* Fingal.　　† Dion.

north

north fide of it immediately commenced the
enemies country; all the nations of the Mœ-
ats, poffeffing from this wall to the friths,
being no lefs at that time enemies than the
Caledonians *. Thus, even according to the
differtator's own account of the matter, Caracalla, after his return with Severus from Caledonia, never faw the Carron nor its banks:

THIS, Sir, being the true ftate of the cafe,
we muft conceive Carachuil foiled and chafed
by Fingal on the banks of the Carron, to have
been, what you know I always took him for,
namely, a very fierce-faced gigantic champion, of the romantic race. By what means,
arts, or powers, he came to be transformed
into the fon of Severus, I have never yet been
able to divine. We are however told †, he
was no other than Caracalla; and on this
fimple arbitrary affertion, utterly repugnant
to the moft authentic monuments ‡, have we
got reared a moft curious new fyftem of hiftory and chronology.

BUT let us proceed with our hero. Fin-

* Dion.　　† Differt. p. 8.　　‡ Comala, p. 87.

gal,

gal, inftead of profecuting his unparallelled
victory over Caracalla, without fo much as
gathering the fpoils, or attempting to reap
the fmalleft advantage to himfelf or his
country; even after Caracalla had not only
fled before him, but left the ifland *; Fingal,
I fay, never minding thefe matters, retreats
with his army towards his capital, performs
certain funeral rites to the memory of Lady
Comala, cafhiers one of his heroes, who had
been the malicious caufe of the unhappy
damfel's death †.

ACCORDING to our tales of the fong, Fingal's next expedition was to Erin. How he
cantoned, or where he encamped his victorious army, what time he took to equip his
naval armament, and embark his brigades;
as to thefe particulars bards are filent, traditions dumb. Our hero, however, gets under fail, arrives with his fleet and army in
Erin ‡, where, at the palace of the great King,
he is moft gracioufly received by his own dear
coufin Cormac MacConar king of all Ireland.
This very coufin Cormac, fay our trufty tra-

* Com.   † Caros.   ‡ Temora.

ditions,

ditions, was at that time upon the point of being overwhelmed, and ftript of his fupreme
dignity, by an inferior Irifh king. This un-
derling king was the fierce Colculla, at the
head of his ferocious Firbolg tribes. With
Colculla and his Firbolg our hero makes very fhort work : " Fingal's fword rofe; Alnecma fled; Fingal returned with fame *."

Our hero has hitherto been very unhappy
in his amours. Now the charming goddefs
begins to fmile. Rofcrana, Princefs-royal of
Erin, falls in love with Fingal. No wonder
fhe did : what lady, though even beyond the
bloom of youth, could well avoid it ? Mac-
Conar gives his daughter to his coufin Fingal, who had juft now faved him from the
Firbolg. Rofcrana conceives a fon, and, in
nature's due time, difclofes to light from
teeming womb the immortal Offian king of
bards.

At the time Offian was born, Fingal was
eighteen years old : Offian at the very fame
age had a fon, whofe name was Ofcar. Ofcar

* Temora.

was

was twenty years old when he acted the heroic part next to his grandfather Fingal against Cairbar.

ALL thefe anecdotes we are favoured with, upon the authority of a very aged, and right reverend tradition, in the laft note on Temora. And according to this reckoning, Fingal turns out juft fifty-fix years old, at the time he flew Cairbar, and obtained his laft glorious victory over the Firbolg tribes.

THIS venerable tradition, if not enfeebled by years, might pretty well fuftain the probable in Fingal's laft achievement, with refpect to his age; the fole purpofe for which it is introduced.

HERE, Sir, permit me to remark, that thefe our Galic traditions are a fort of two-edged weapons, and require to be wielded with great attention, and a very fteady hand : for, as the probable, by this circumftance of the hero's age, is, in one point of view, well fuftained in his laft exploit; fo, by means of this, and other circumftances, is the probable

quite

quite obfcured, and utterly loft in the more great and glorious achievements afcribed to Fingal before his marriage with Rofcrana. This, Sir, is the place where this tradition obliges us to trace our hero's fteps backwards for fome paces.

PRIOR to this happy event of his marriage, Fingal had muftered an army, equipped a fleet, failed from Morven to Erin, faced an e-nemy numerous and fierce, and finally gain-ed a decifive victory, and won the triumphal fpoils.

FOR all, and each of thefe operations, a probable allotment of time muft be affigned.

FOR the moft wonderful of all Fingal's wondrous victories, that, I mean, over Cara-calla and his Roman army, the time taken up in preparing the means, muftering the force for carrying this immortal enterprife into ex-ecution, a probable number of days is de-manded.

WHAT number of weeks intervened be-

C   twixt

twixt the commencement of Fingal's prepa-
rations for this laſt ſignal event, and the time
he feaſted with Sarno in Iniſtore?

How long prior to this feaſting-match in
Iniſtore, was the day when all Lochlin fled
or died before our hero, at the windy-halls
of Gormal?

From this diſtinguiſhed exploit at Gormal, how far back are we to ſet the time of
Starno's defeat by Fingal in Morven?

When theſe times and intervals are aſſign-
ed, we have, you know, the hero's age in each
achievement, and of conſequence may readily
pronounce with regard to the probable in this
reſpect. But the epic heroic muſe is obliged
to maintain her probable, not only in regard
to her hero's age, but likewiſe in ſeveral other
points of view; in the means, force, and effort, by which the enterpriſe is finally achieved: and when the events appear grand, and
thick crouded one on the back of another,
the fields of action far diſtant, the ſeas ſtormy,
navigation little underſtood, ſhipping ſcarce,

roads

roads not very practicable, as seems, in every particular, to have been the case in Fingal's antenuptial achievements; in such circumstances, not only a probability must be sustained in time, force, and effort, for carrying the enterprise into execution; but also a probability in time, means, and method, for transporting the hero and his force from one field of action to the other, and that in proportion to their respective distances, and difficulty of passage, &c.

THUS, Sir, as the forequoted tradition has done some service at one end; so has it, I begin to fear, done much mischief at the other; as now the heroic probable, in these most splendid exploits of Fingal's early youth, seems quite to vanish from mortal ken.

PRAY, Sir, as this is a capital article, and bids fair to ascertain the true nature and genius of our epic Galic poems, and finally to determine with regard to the species of poetry in which they ought to be ranged, let us to our attention add patience, in order to determine this important point; let us, I say, resume, and be fully explicit.

IN

In the beginning of the third century, Fingal King of Morven vanquiſhed in battle, and made priſoner Starno King of Denmark, who had with a fleet and army invaded the north-weſt of Scotland, where Fingal then reigned.

Some time after this, Fingal, invited by Starno, ſails from the north-weſt of Scotland to Denmark; keeps on his armour of ſteel; makes all Denmark flee or die. Fingal, from this achievement in Denmark, ſails back to the north-weſt of Scotland, buries the body of Agandecca.

Fingal next repairs by ſea, or land, or both, as you pleaſe, to the Orkneys; feaſts with Sarno, who then reigned over theſe iſlands.

From the Orkneys, Fingal ſails back to the north-weſt of Scotland, and ſomewhere thereabout raiſes, muſters, and marches an army of his ſubjects, to the banks of Carron water, where with this army he defeats, and chaſes Caracalla, ſon to the Roman Emperor Severus,

Severus, supported by a whole veteran Roman army.

FINGAL, after this victory over Caracalla and his Roman army, marches back to the north-weft of Scotland, the place we do not pretend to afcertain, and there equips a fleet, tranfports an army to Ireland, vanquifhes and kills in battle·Colculla, a mighty Irifh prince, fupported by a numerous army.

ALL thefe exploits has Fingal achieved before his marriage with Rofcrana; that is, by the time he was feventeen years three months old *.

IN the firft exploit, befides that of the hero's age, appears an utter improbability, in every other point of view.

IT is utterly improbable, that Starno, or any other King of Denmark, in that age, poffeffed the means, arts, or powers of invading Britain, acrofs the ftormy intervening feas.

* Temora.

IT

IT is not, with me, very probable, that
the King of Lochlin, the means and powers
fuppofed, would then have invaded the barren,
defert mountains of Morven. What! can you
figure, Sir, could he expect to find there ? To
the feaft of fhells he could not expect an in-
vitation, a hoftile and bloody invader as he
came ; he muft then go a-climbing the mountains, and hunting the deer; or, inftead of
gathering from Morven's hills the expences
of his expedition, return to Gormal, without
fo much as one morfel of venifon for all
his trouble. Nor, in this firft exploit, can I
difcover any probability in the means, force,
and effort by which it was achieved. The
only probability appearing to me, is, that the
bard, whoever he was, drew from the ideas
of the romance; and that, in this manner,
he has fucceeded to a marvel, in holding up
to us his beardlefs Fingal a romantic champ-
pion of the firft magnitude in prowefs as in
courtefy.

IN Fingal's fecond achievement the fame
improbability evidently appears. It is utterly improbable that the Kings of Morven
were,

were, in thefe days, in the practice of going
to Denmark, in order to feaft upon invita-
tion. It is utterly improbable they were
poffeffed of the means and arts for fuch expeditions. And, after we have fuppofed our
hero at the court of Denmark, there is the
fame utter improbability in the force and effort, by means of which all Lochlin fled, or
died before him; nothing here to fupport a-
ny degree of the probable, but that Fingal
kept on his arms of fteel; and, unlefs we
fuppofe thefe arms utterly inchanted, an utter improbability recurs; even though we
add twenty years to our hero's age.

In this fecond exploit again evidently appears mother Romance, and her invincible fon
the moft courteous knight; a feafting-match;
the affections of a young princefs won; all
the moft mighty champions of a whole nation made to flee, or die, in a manner fo marvellous; the bloody and favage tragedy of the
lovely and loving damfel's death; the invincible prowefs of the Galic hero, in carrying
off her body, maugre all the power of Lochlin; his refined courtefy in conveying the
                                    lifelefs

lifelefs corfe of his unhappy miſtreſs aboard his white-failed fhip, and tranſporting the fame to Morven's kingdom, and there piouſly performing funeral rites; with me, Sir, all theſe bear fuch ſtriking marks of the Romance and her knight, that I have always wondered how they could be miſtaken.

FINGAL's exploits third and fourth, as our traditions have coupled them together, we ſhall take jointly under our review.

IN Fingal's expedition to a feaſting-match in the Orkneys, appear the fame ſtriking improbabilities as in that to Denmark.

IN his victory over Caracalla and the Ro-man army on the Carron, there is firſt a plain impoſſibility; for this very plain reaſon, that no Caracalla, no Roman army was at that time there: and fuppoſing Caracalla was fo impertinently officious, as to march at the head of his father's army, from the fouth of the Northumbrian wall to the banks of the Carron, to retard or prevent Fingal's intend-ed match with the Princeſs of Iniſtore; an

utter

utter improbability rifes to view, in the force
and effort by which this immortal victory is
obtained : for, according to our epic Galic
mufe, our hero defeats and chafes a Roman
general, and a veteran victorious army, in as
fhort time, with as little effort, no adequate
force appearing, — as one inchanted champion, in the romance, foils and chafes his rival
champion — a Fingal, a Carachuil.

AGAIN, Comala, charmed at her royal father's feaft, Comala, difguifed in armour as a
young warriour, following her deareft charmer,
the young King of Morven, acrofs feas, friths,
and mountains, from the Orkneys, to the
banks of the Carron, difplays to view the
moft genuine features of romantic chivalry.

I AM forry, Sir, I fhould be obliged, in
this affair of Princefs Comala, to condemn
our moft courteous hero, as deeply deficient in
point of courtefy. It was, in my humble
opinion, neither courteous nor genteel, nay,
nor even very manly, in Fingal, to leave the
amiable loving ftranger Comala, now fo far
from her royal father's houfe, on a hill at fome

D   diftance

diftance from the battle, under colour, for-
footh, of a fniveling pretence, that he could
not find time to marry her!—In this my hear-
ty cenfure I fhall, no doubt, be joined by
every lady of fpirit, every well-bred gentleman. For we have ground to believe, that
the ritual of the Caledonian church did not,
in thofe days, ftrictly require any great length
of time, or extent of ceremonial form, in order to admit the Monarch to the embraces of
the Lady he had chofen for his royal con-
fort.

THE Caledonians, you know, in thefe times,
had their wives in common. Of this ancient practice among them, this their focial
difpofition, this their matrimonial freedom,
the fmart repartee made in vindication thereof *, about this very time, by the Caledonian
Lady to the Roman Emprefs, ftands a lafting
monument. Our Gal.c ber , on the contrary, holds up his heroes wooing and charming their damfels; winning and efpoufing their
dames with the very quinteffence of knightly
courtefy; and his ladies won by their gal-

* Dion.

lants,

lants, given in marriage by their princely fathers ; and, after their efpoufals, affecting a ftarched decency of ceremonial, and high degree of romantic decorum; all much more refembling the more hallowed-like Galic times, pofterior to the days of the good St Patrick, and holy St Colomb, than the natural naked manners, and bare-arfed behaviour of the ancient Caledonians. .

Don't you think, Sir, it is highly ominous, if not quite decifive, againft the affumed antiquity of our Galic poems, that, thro' the whole of them, there is not marked, in one fingle inftance, any ot the known diftinguifhed cuftoms, any of the characteriftical manners, arts, arms, &c. of the brave ancient Caledonians, during the very age in which our Galic bard, as is pretended, fung ? — All thefe has the light of Galic fong quite reverfed.

Return we now, Sir, to our probabilities. In Fingal's fifth achievement, that in Erin, there appears an utter improbability in the

D 2   means,

means, arts, and implements for building and equipping his fleet.

In his victory over Colculla, there is no shadow of probability in the force and effort exerted in gaining the battle, and killing the mighty hostile Prince. " On this field of " action, Fingal's sword rose, Alnecma fled, " Colculla fell."

Pray, Sir, have we here one grain of probability, but what we can pick from the occult qualities of our hero's sword? May not FINGAL, on this occasion, be called, with some propriety, THE KNIGHT OF THE INCHANTED SWORD?

But, before we leave these immortal achievements of our hero's early youth, let us throw a little of our attention towards times and circumstances.

At the time that Severus, with the greatest Roman army Britain ever saw, is forcing his way thro' bogs and mountains, and over-running all Caledonia; at this very time the mighty Fingal, the most invincible of Caledonian he-

rocs,

roes, is not fo much as heard of in his native
land! —he is elfe where; —he is engaged in
exploits more fublime! —

FINGAL is at this time far from home,
feafting, combating, charming, and, alas,
burying the ladies * ! On this occafion, the
moft important, the moft interefting to Caledonia, and all her braveft fons, we muft call
for Fingal King of Morven at the windy-halls
of Gormal, or at the court of Sarno King of
the Orkneys.

AMID fuch variety of exploits of Fingal's
early youth, one itfelf, pretty remarkable, had
almoft efcaped me. — We have it from Fingal's own mouth; and it appears, to me however, to indicate very clearly the true fpecies
and quality of Fingal's heroifm; and, no lefs
clearly, to difplay the true genius and fpirit of
Offian's poetry.

FINGAL, during his war with Swaran in
Ireland †, is pleafed to vaunt, to his gallant
grandfon Ofcar, the heroic deeds of his own

---

* Agandecca. Temora.   † Fingal, book 3.

youth.

youth. " My arm," fays he, " was the fup-
" port of the injured, and the weak refted
" behind the lightning of my fteel." He fets
before Ofcar an inftance of his gallant and
courteous heroifm. He tells him, that one
day, as he returned from Cona's heath, a
white-failed boat appeared; in the boat was
Fainafollis, the daughter of Craca's King.
This lady, in her white-failed boat, had fled
from the Shetland iflands to Morven, acrofs the
ftormy intervening feas, in order to claim the
protection of our moft courteous, yet beardlefs hero, againft Borbar King of Sora, in •
Scandinavia, her ftormy and uncourteous
lover.

The Lady gets on fhore; declares to Fingal the caufe of her coming. — Our hero moft
courteoufly undertakes her fecurity. — " Reft
" thou," fays he, " behind my fhield; reft
" in peace, thou beam of light!"

In the mean time Borbar's fhip appears;
" his mafts high bended o'er the fea, behind
" their fheets of fnow." Borbar's fhip comes
to land. Fingal, without ufing any means,
friendly

friendly or hoftile, for the fecurity of the unhappy princefs, not fo much as interpofing
the promifed protection of his fhield, with
more courtefy than true judgment, in my
humble opinion, invites Borbar to partake
the feaft. Sora's ftormy King, regardlefs of
courteous ceremony, draws his bow. The
haplefs Fainafollis, King Fingal's royal ward,
as fhe ftands trembling by our hero's fide, falls
dead by Borbar's fhaft. Fingal at laft, perhaps a little too late, draws his fword; Borbar finks beneath his mighty arm. Morven's
King lays in two tombs of ftone the haplefs
lovers of youth.

PRAY, Sir, had Fingal, do you really think,
any great reafon to vaunt his heroifm in this
exploit?

To me it has always appeared an opera-
tion hugely bungled. Our hero, on this unhappy occafion, performs not near fo well as
he promifes. His victory over Caracalla and
his ever victorious Roman army, had he been
bleffed with any remembrance thereof, would,
according

according to my opinion, have been a much brighter model for Ofcar's imitation.

THIS odd tale, however, of Craca's fun-beam, juft as we have feen it, I prefume to hold up as a very ftriking fpecimen of the wildeft extravagance of the romantic mufe.

FINGAL, Sir, we have now viewed on all fides, in every light; — and, upon the moft impartial fcrutiny, have been able to difcover nothing like the true epic hero: — but every the moft ftriking mark of the romantic cham-pion we have clearly feen; — in manners, amours, deeds of courteous chivalry;—time, place, and every attitude, in every achieve-ment. — We have feen his exploits far above his years, in themfelves more than wonder-ful; — in force, effort, time, place, and every circumftance, — utterly devoid of the epic he-roic probable.

BUT, Sir, let us not be difcouraged. —If in thefe tales of the times of other years, we can-not difcover a probable of one kind, of ano-ther perhaps we may. For, from thefe Galic

lic poems, have I learned to diftinguifh the epic heroic mufe from the epic romantic, or epic Galic.

THE epic heroic mufe has, you know, her own fupernatural machinery, by means of which fhe fuftains a fpecies of probability peculiar to her, in whatever action or incident highly marvellous fhe is difpofed to fing.

THE epic romantic, or epic Galic mufe has, in like manner, her proper fupernatural machinery, fpells, charms, inchantments, and many other necromantic powers; all thefe enter into the compofition of her machinery; upborn by thefe, deeds fhe fings of higheft wonder, deeds far beyond the ken of natural powers! in wonder fhe delights, in wonder fhe abounds : wonder, Sir, appears to me the very life and foul of the epic Galic mufe. That fhe is mighty folicitous with regard to the probable, 1 dare not aver : yet does fhe maintain a fpecies of probability, fuited to her nature and genius, when not bereft of her proper machinery.

E   IN

IN the epic Galic poems under our review, nothing, it is true, of this machinery appears; hence it is, that in them we are fo much at a lofs with regard to the probable.

WHAT fhall we imagine, Sir, has become of our machinery? Has it, perhaps, been withdrawn or fecreted by fome kind but erring hand? Whatever may be in this, we have feen it much wanted on all our great occafions. Let us now, pray, contraft thefe tales of the fong with the authentic hiftory of thofe times, in order, if poffible, to inveftigate the true æra of compofition.

THIS new traditional fyftem, with all the generofity of the moft courteous Fingalic fpirit, beftows upon the ancient Caledonians heavy mails of fteel, fcull-caps of the fame folid metal, banners inlaid with ftones and gold, and chariot-harnefs bright ftudded with gems *, &c. The Roman hiftorians, informed by ocular evidence, roundly affert they had no fuch thing †. Thefe Caledonians, fay they, had no other arms than long pointlefs

* Temora.   † Tacitus. Dion.

fwords,

íwords, light pikes, daggers, fmall targets; and inftead of reprefenting them covered over with fteel, as Trenmor in Denmark, and the champions in the days of chivalry, explicitly declare *, that thefe Caledonians fought naked, and were utter ftrangers to corflet or helmet of any kind whatever.

FOR this deficiency, however, on the Roman fide, we have luckily hit on a remedy; we can fetch all the other heavy accoutrements, and fplendid array, from the machinery of our epic Galic mufe.

THE light of fong, with all that romantic benignity of heart, which fhines fo confpicuoufly in the works of our royal bard, endues the Caledonians with towers †, fhaded walls, ftone palaces, golden arrows, fhells ftudded with gems, and kindly indulges them in frequent feafts, caroufals, tournaments.

THE ancient hiftorians, writing of this people in the fame age, on the contrary in-

* Herodian.   † Fingal.

form

form us *, that their habitations were no better than huts or cabins; that their viands confifted in venifon, the milk and flefh of their cattle, fruits, herbs, roots, and bark of trees.

HISTORY, it is true, fupplies us with one fpecies more of Caledonian viands; which, if properly underftood, with the help of a little fkill in French cookery, might have been made to pafs pretty well for the feaft of fhells.

FOR Solma's towers, palaces, golden arrows, &c. our machinery muft again be called in aid:

OUR epic Galic mufe affigns to her Caledonians, even as high as the firft century, white-failed fhips; reprefents them as fcudding over the waves of wide tempeftuous feas, with more eafe and lefs danger than what is known from experience to be the cafe to this very day †.

---

* Dion.   † Fingal.

THE

THE light of Galic fong has equipped, for them fleets, formidable armaments; eftablifh-ed for them a conftant intercourfe, and current, communication, fometimes friendly; fometimes hoftile, with Denmark, and every part of Scandinavia, &c. Fingal, his fons, grandfons, heroes; all thefe, according to our epic Galic mufe, repair, in their white-failed dark-bofomed fhips, to Carecthura, Gormal, Sora, and every place in the Scandinavian realms, with as current frequency, and with all the feeming eafe, that attends the moft mighty champions-errant in their movements from caftle to caftle, from vale to vale!

OUR heroes and thofe champions have operations and exploits perfectly, fimilar, and both return from their equally romantic expeditions, equally covered over with the fame romantic fame. This article of fhipping and fleets in the poffeffion of the Caledonians, in thofe rude, artlefs, and early times, appeared, you know, to me, at firft fight, decifive with regard to the æra of compofition.

HISTORY

HISTORY fays nothing like this, gives not the leaft hint of the exiftence of one fingle bark, or fifher-boat, in any place all around both Caledonia, and the country of the Mœats; which, as has been obferved, extended from the friths to the Northumbrian wall.

HAD there been any fuch thing in thefe nations, can we imagine the Roman hiftorians would have omitted it? No more, it is prefumed, than they would have neglected to mention their heavy armour, their mails of fteel, had thefe appeared among the Caledonians. For the better the vanquifhed had been provided with the means and implements of defence, the greater glory accrued to the victors.

THIS article of fhipping and fleets I deem abfolutely incompatible with the known fituation, circumftances, and artlefs ftate of this rude people in thofe times.

CAN we, Sir, figure a people that has not yet attained art, culture, or induftry fufficient

cient to rear a houfe above a hut, to till a
fingle acre, reap a fingle fhock, provide themfelves with coat or fhoe *, at the fame time
building fhips, equipping fleets, navigating
feas, feas dangerous to modern art and im-
provement in failing? A fleet of white-failed
fhips, conftructed and equipped by a people
in fuch circumftances, may, methinks, be
fafely pronounced a rare phenomenon; or ra-
ther a real prodigy, not to be parallelled in
hiftory. But in our Galic poems, every one
muft obferve, there is feldom any juft proportion maintained in the caufe to the ef-
fect.

THE fingle circumftance of the Roman
walls, do not you think, Sir, by itfelf fufficient to give the negative in this article?

HAD any Caledonian prince, in the third
century, been poffeffed of fleets, fuch as Fingal is fancied then to have had, thefe walls
had nothing availed the Romans.

THE Caledonians from Cantire, or any part

* Dion.

of Argylefhire, might, in a few hours, have landed in Airfhire; thus the wall betwixt the friths became of no ufe. Was the Caledonian difpofed to ftretch a little farther, he doubled the Northumbrian wall, and in confequence it was rendered equally unavailing againft the invaders.

The fame reafoning muft hold with refpect to fhipping and fleets on the caft fide of Caledonia: and on this fide, methinks, we might naturally expect firft to find them. Whether Morven's kingdom, without ftrong extraneous aids, could, even to this day, have produced fuch fleets, may, it is humbly prefumed, bear a queftion. Whatever may be in this, it is a full hundred years after Fingal's laft expedition to Ireland, before the time when we find any ground in hiftory to believe, the Caledonians had got art enough to furnifh out fome corroughs fufficient to waft a parcel of the boldeft of them acrofs the Clyde below Dumbarton.

The whole weight of this heavy article muft therefore be thrown upon the fupernatural

tural powers of our machinery, there to reſt and remain, till the learned gentlemen patrons of our romantic tales, can find leiſure to pro‑ duce, within the limits of Morven's kingdom, at any time during the three firſt centuries, natural cauſes adequate to ſuch effects.

ANOTHER conſideration, Sir, I deem no leſs deciſive àgainſt the aſſumed antiquity of the epic Galic poems; namely, the frequent invaſions from Denmark, and wars of the ſea with that nation.

IN the tales of wonder ſung by our Galic muſe *, we find Starno King of Denmark in‑ vading Morven with a fleet and army, much about the time Severus entered and over-run Caledonia. The bards in Comala ſing, " Our " delight will be in the wars of the ocean, " and our hands red in the blood of Loch‑ " lin," &c.

WE have no ground in hiſtory, as little in the nature of the thing, to believe that the Lochlinites were further advanced in cul‑

* Fingal.

F ture,

ture, arts, &c. during thofe times, than the Caledonians: in confequence, they were equally devoid of the means and powers of making invafions. Befides, hiftorians, you know, agree in fixing the firft invafion of this ifland from that quarter, to the latter end of the eighth century *. It was in that age Charles the Great bore very hard upon the Heathen Saxons; he compelled them to profefs the Chriftian religion, or expelled them their country. The moft obftinate in their old faith, and former way of life, withdrew northward, joined themfelves with the then inhabitants of Denmark, &c. and taught them the art of bark-building, and practice of courfing by fea. Hence the æra of our poems is inferred pofterior to the eighth century.

ONCE more, Sir, thefe Galic poems, as we have feen, are evidently replete with all the ideas of chivalry, its manners, arms, amours; replete with all the fuper-refined courtefy, and fantaftic affectations of the romance. In all thefe our Galic champions fuperabound; Fingal in particular.

* A. D. 787.

CHAMPIONS

CHAMPIONS covered over with ſteel; prin-
ceſſes inſtigated by love, and an eager fondneſs
of being diſcovered in the ſame knightly array, challenging thoſe heroes to combat; as
Trenmor and Inibacca at the court of Denmark; carouſals interluded with tournaments; the extreme politeneſs of giving the
choice in the combat; ladies enamoured, diſ-
guiſed in armour as warriours, following the
invincible charming champions acroſs ſeas,
friths, mountains, wilds; as Comala follows
Fingal from the Orkney iſlands to the Carron
in Stirlingſhire; the hideous delicacy of allowing an unfortunate princeſs to die of pure
love, from mere want of matrimony, after
ſuch immenſe trouble, ſuch ardent deſire as
the unhappy Comala beſtowed on our ſuper-
refined Fingal; royal damſels flying, in white-
ſailed boats, acroſs ſtormy ſeas, in order to
claim the protection of courteous champions
againſt their ſtormy and uncourteous lovers;
as the hapleſs and ill-protected Fainaſollis
flies before Borbar Sora's King, to the protection of our moſt courteous Fingal.

OF all and each of theſe wild romantic

fancies,

fancies, not the fmalleft traces, not a fingle
veftige, I dare affirm, can be made appear ex-
ifting in the manners, ideas, or poetry of this
country, anterior to the Norman conqueft.

ALL thefe whimfical embellifhments of
the romantic mufe, I deem to have been im-
ported from the continent by the lordly con-
querors; not all at once, perhaps, but piece-
meal, and in progrefs of time. What number of years it might require to tranfplant
thefe deemed exotics, from the fouth end of
Britain, into the kingdom of Morven; what
time more for their ftriking root under its
bleak mountains; their growing up to per-
fection in this ftrange foil and clime; their
difplaying their mature and gliftering fruits,
mingled with the light of the Galic fong:
what length of time may reafonably be
allowed for all and each of thefe happy
events, I fhall not prefume precifely to determine. For the laft fhining event, if my con-
jecture may be fuftained, I would incline to
allot, at fooneft, the thirteenth century.

THUS, Sir, have I ventured to curtail the
years

years of our epic Galic fongs by one full thou-
fand : and, I verily believe, for their real be-
nefit, their trueft intereft. They are ftill
abundantly aged to tread firm, when depri-
ved of ftaff or hold; ftill of too many years
to ftand fteady the fupporting pillars under
any weight of hiftorical ftructure.

In thefe our poems, whatever their age
may be, have we feen reverfed every characteriftical idea, given us by the Roman hiftorians, of the ancient Caledonians; in manners,
cuftoms, arts, arms, and whole train of life,
during the three firft centuries, the very period in which our heroes are faid to have
acted, and our bard to have fung.

Hence may we not, with the greateft ju-
ftice, infer, that the original authors, bards,
talemakers, or by whatever name they may
be called, were utter ftrangers to Caledonia,
and the moft important and interefting events
which happened in her very bowels during
this fame period ?

Whether the gentlemen patrons of our
Galic

Galic poems have been, in any great degree, more attentive to this period of Caledonian hiſtory, than the original authors were knowing therein, I do not preſume to ſay; you, Sir, can better judge.

To adopt theſe ſongs and traditions for any thing like hiſtory, I would incline abſolutely to refuſe; and that for many reaſons appearing to me very good. At preſent I ſhall confine myſelf to one, which is furniſhed by the gentleman who gave theſe poems to the public. He rejects, with ſeeming diſdain, the authority of the Iriſh hiſtorians *; becauſe, ſays he, theſe gentlemen are ſaid, if not to create facts, to adopt, however, the traditions of their bards for real facts.

Is not this, Sir, preciſely his own caſe? Has he favoured us with any one voucher for his facts, highly romantic in themſelves, and repugnant to all genuine monuments, as they are; beſide the traditions of his bards, reinforced indeed by other traditions, venerable,

* Fingal.

vulgar

vulgar traditions, of above fifteen centuries old ?

THE fneer thrown on the Irifh gentle-men, I am afraid, recoils.

THAT the patrons of this new traditional hiftory have created facts, I do not fay ; that they have extracted facts, huge facts, from founds, to me appears an obvious truth. Of this, Sir, I offer one fhining inftance. From the fingle word *Carac-huil*, obvioufly the fictitious name of a romantic champion, have they not had the art and addrefs to extract the fon of a Roman Emperor at the head of a mighty army, and alfo a moft glorious vic-tory gained over this Roman general, and his mighty army, *A. D.* 210, on the banks of the Carron, by FINGAL King of Morven ?

F I N I S.

www.ingramcontent.com/pod-product-compliance
Lightning Source LLC
Chambersburg PA
CBHW021557270326
41931CB00009B/1255